**I'd like to thank my fellow Picture & Word students, my professors and mentors—
April Prince, Judy Sue Goodwin Sturges, Colleen, and Ms. Deverie—Jessie, Andrew,
and the rest of my family back home for giving me the support, love, and
encouragement I needed to make this book. A special thank you to
Eileen Robinson and Kristen Nobles for making this book come to life.
—S. R.**

At publication, all URLs in this book were accurate.
Charlesbridge and the author are not responsible for the content of any website.

Charlesbridge · 9 Galen Street, Watertown, MA 02472 · www.charlesbridge.com

Library of Congress Cataloging-in-Publication Data
Names: Rodriguez, Sylvia, author.
Title: Black hair can: the roots of our roots / Sylvia Rodriguez.
Description: Watertown, MA: Charlesbridge, 2025. | Audience: Ages 4–8. | Audience: Grades K–1. |
Summary: By tracing Black ethnic hairstyles from their origins in Africa to the
contemporary United States, this book shows how hair can be important
to one's self-esteem and identity.—Provided by publisher.
Identifiers: LCCN 2024033009 (print) | LCCN 2024033010 (ebook) |
ISBN 9781623545901 (hardcover) | ISBN 9781632894595 (ebook)
Subjects: LCSH: Hairdressing—Africa—History—Juvenile literature. |
Hairdressing of African Americans—History—Juvenile literature. |
Self-esteem—Juvenile literature. | Identity—Juvenile literature.
Classification: LCC GT2295.A35 R63 2025 (print) | LCC GT2295.A35 (ebook) |
DDC 391.5089/96—dc23/eng/20240922
LC record available at https://lccn.loc.gov/2024033009
LC ebook record available at https://lccn.loc.gov/2024033010

Printed in China · OPIC
(hc) 10 9 8 7 6 5 4 3 2 1

Illustrations created digitally
Text type set in Katrina
Edited by Eileen Robinson
Designed by Kristen Nobles
Production supervised by Jennifer Most Delaney

BLACK HAIR CAN

The Roots of Our Roots

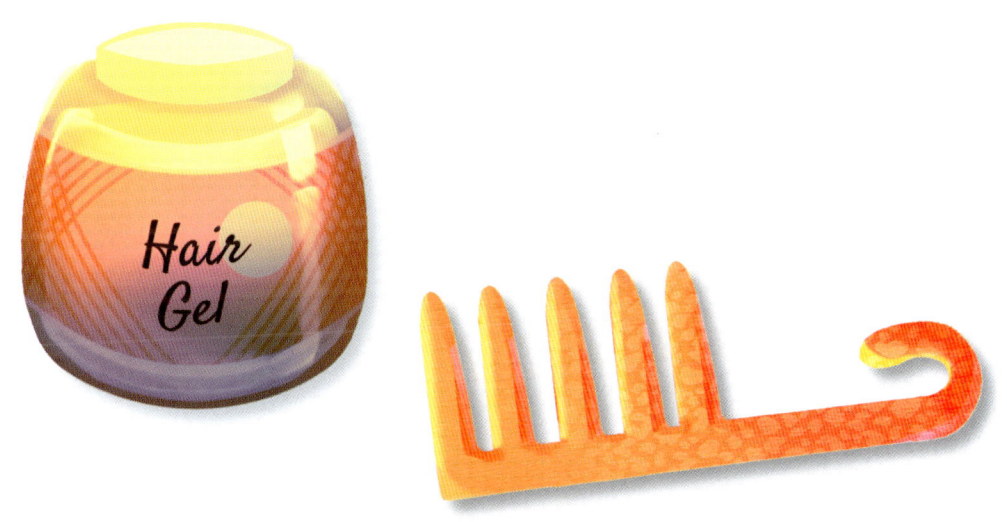

Sylvia Rodriguez

ᵢᵣᵢ Charlesbridge

Black hair is rooted deep in history.

There is no other ethnic group whose hair is so connected with its identity. It is a symbol of empowerment, self-preservation, and individualism.

BLACK HAIR CAN

*be a way to remember
and honor ancestors.*

BLACK HAIR CAN

*reflect someone's inner (ewa-inu)
and outer (ewa-ode) beauty.*

BLACK HAIR CAN

be a connection

to a spiritual world, or orisha.

BLACK HAIR CAN

be a crown:

ornate, decorative, and delicate.

BLACK HAIR CAN

be elaborate,

a mosaic of geometry

and patterns.

BLACK HAIR CAN

*be carefully shaped and formed,
fluid and majestic.*

BLACK HAIR CAN

be an indication of

status in society.

BLACK HAIR CAN

forge a path

toward a new life.

BLACK HAIR CAN

be hidden and protected,
covered but loved.

BLACK HAIR CAN

be a symbol of

pride, power,

and freedom.

BLACK HAIR CAN

be a form of protest,
untouched and natural.

BLACK HAIR IS

a culture, a community,

and a collaboration

of past and present.

"The CROWN Act was created in 2019 by Dove and the CROWN Coalition, in partnership with then State Senator Holly J. Mitchell of California."

—*Dove, CROWN Coalition*

The CROWN Act

What is the CROWN Act?

The CROWN Act is a campaign to keep young girls and women safe and protected from discrimination because of their hair's texture or the form, shape, or style they choose to wear it in.

Why do we need the CROWN Act?

From age five to adulthood, young girls and women endure direct commentary and micro-aggressions directed toward their hair, affecting their self-esteem and sense of identity among their peers and in the world.

This is systemic and has an impact on their ability to live rich lives when they cannot be or express themselves.

What does CROWN stand for?

Creating a
Respectful and
Open
World for
Natural hair

NOTE TO READERS

You should NEVER feel you have to change the style or texture of your hair to be accepted.

Your hair is a symbol of empowerment, self-preservation, and individualism.

Your hair is remarkable. Whether you choose to be with it or without it, the choice is yours and yours alone.

The Roots of Our Roots

 Black hair has a very rich history and begins in the root of Black culture: Africa. The continent is home to various cultures and communities with ancestry going back thousands and thousands of years. Hair shaped communities often in very drastic ways.

With thousands of tribes spread across vast, diverse lands, it can be difficult to find a starting place to root Black hair's place in history, but one can start by looking at some of the most ancient tribes—the Yoruba, Zulu, and Igbo people.

 Often, Yoruba hairstyles represent class and sometimes historical events, and are even adapted from their ancient representations to modern counterparts, such as the shuku hairstyle.

Yoruba people reside mainly in the southern part of Nigeria, with some scattered populations in Togo and Benin.

The shuku (or suku) hairstyle involves braiding a bump on top of the head, often that of a woman. Historically, it was typically reserved for wives of royalty but is now often worn by women of all backgrounds, including young schoolgirls. Variations of this hairstyle include the suku sesema, suku na poi, suku elegbe, and suku onididi.

 Styles such as the dada hairstyle can be tied to religion and spirituality.

Some Yoruba people believed that thick, dense natural hair was of spiritual importance, so many parents refrained from cutting their children's hair for fear of death or illness. Their matted hair grew into long dreadlocks. This resulted in the children being called dada. Dada are considered to have special capabilities, and their hair is a direct connection to the spirits. Dreadlocks were associated with the orisha (god) Olukun, the ruler of all bodies of water and other water gods.

 Well-known for their elaborate hairstyles, the Igbo people have a particularly ornate and decorative look known as ojongo. It is an intricate crest decorated with various materials, including feathers, bone, wood, shells, beads, and money.

 A popular hairstyle worn today by Black people, Bantu knots come from the Zulu, a South African cultural group that has some ties with the Swazi and Xhosa peoples. Bantu knots are characterized by multiple clean, typically triangular, sections of the hair with the hair "knotted" around itself in each section to form a spiral.

 In Rwanda, the Tutsi and Hutu people wore a hairstyle known as amasunzu, which is more than five hundred years old. It involves making curved shapes in the Afro-textured hair by cutting it into shape from the side and middle of the head and allowing it to grow in that form. This style was worn among nobles, and many villages would compete to see who could make the best designs!

 One popular hairstyle today, known as Fulani braids, comes from the Fulani people of West Africa. Dating back thousands of years, the hairstyle was a symbol of identity among African women.

The hair is parted and braided down the middle, and the sides of the head are adorned with many small rows or "cornrows" braided directly to the head.

 Sadly, because of American slavery and European colonization, there is a loss of culture associated with the treacherous journey that was the Middle Passage. While being transported in the crowded, inhumane, unhygienic quarters of slave trade ships, kidnapped African people had their hair shaved or cut to remove important aspects of their identity and strip them of both their humanity and their culture.

 Cornrows, resembling rows of corn in a field or on a plantation, were a common hairstyle worn by enslaved people as a means of communication. They were commonly used as maps that showed escape routes. Many enslaved African people were not allowed to learn to read, and it was unsafe to communicate with written words in any way. Some had rice and seeds braided into their hair as nourishment for escapes or even just for daily life, as they were not given substantial meals.

 Prior to slavery, bandannas, scarves, and head-wraps were commonly used to protect the head. Many Haitian women who journeyed across the ocean in search of a better life in the United States wore headwraps.

In vodun religion, which is still followed today in places like Haiti and Nigeria, the head is very important and symbolizes someone's personality so protecting it is vital.

 In Jamaica, musician Bob Marley became a prominent figure in the pro-Black Rastafarian movement started by activist Marcus Garvey.

Dreadlocks became synonymous with Rastafarianism, with Marley writing and performing songs about the culture and specifically about the hairstyle. Dreadlocks are characterized by thick, Afro-textured hair being allowed to mat—meaning they usually aren't brushed out but are allowed to tangle—and form long, thick, rope-like structures.

 At the height of the Civil Rights Movement, many Black people let their hair grow out as a means of protest and empowerment. With the rise of the hot comb, it became common to straighten ethnic hair to appear more "professional" in mainly white work environments. White bosses, coworkers, and peers saw natural hair as unkempt and dirty. Wearing it out in its untouched state was in direct protest to white mainstream America.

Afros, or giant, beautiful, shapely spheres of hair, danced among the heads of Black people. Their hair was carefully picked with combs to increase the volume of their curly locks.

 Synthetic hair was used as far back as ancient Egypt. It was common for royalty and rulers to wear wigs or weaves. The more extravagant your extensions, the more rich or important you were.

Wigs were created by ancient Egyptians to shield those with shaven, bald heads from the hot sun and were held in place using beeswax and resin. Men would often shave their heads to wear wigs, and women would usually have their hair braided for weaves to show off their wealth. A weave is excess hair not attached to the head, often bought in bundles, that is sewn to braided hair to resemble a full head of hair without using one's natural hair. Cleopatra, for example, was said to have weaves made out of sheep wool and human hair.

Many weaves today use hair that comes from places in East Asia, and the industry is incredibly large and diverse. Hair in weaves can be curly, straight, wavy, and more.

 Modern hairstyles across the African diaspora, including those in the United States, have strong roots in African ancestry, and many are adapted and transformed as trends change. They are a symbol of Black pride and of the perseverance of a culture that was taken away and altered.